Alfred's

P9-CRU-406

I P A
Made Easy

A Guidebook for the
International Phonetic Alphabet

By Anna Wentlent

Alfred Music
P.O. Box 10003
Van Nuys, CA 91410-0003
alfred.com

ISBN-10: 1-4706-1561-4
ISBN-13: 978-1-4706-1561-1

Table of Contents

VOWELS

CONSONANTS

Visit the online Listening Lab at **alfred.com/ipamadeeasy**
to hear recorded demonstrations of every sound.

VOWELS

[a]

forward vowel

American English speakers are most familiar with this bright "ah" vowel sound as the beginning of a diphthong; however, the isolated sound can be approximated by very slowly saying the word "by." The first vowel sound—before the tongue moves—is [a].

English	Italian
n/a	c<u>a</u>r<u>a</u>
French	**Latin**
l<u>à</u>	n/a
German	**Spanish**
w<u>a</u>nn	boc<u>a</u>

 Listening Lab: Example #1

4

back vowel

Keep the jaw relaxed when pronouncing this dark "ah" vowel sound.

English	Italian
f<u>a</u>ther	n/a
French	**Latin**
ch<u>â</u>teau	<u>a</u>ve
German	**Spanish**
k<u>a</u>m	c<u>a</u>ro

Listening Lab: Example #2

[æ]

forward vowel

Keep the lips parted and the jaw relaxed. American English speakers often spread the lips horizontally; however, that is not necessary to produce the correct vowel sound.

English	Italian
c<u>a</u>t	n/a
French	**Latin**
n/a	n/a
German	**Spanish**
n/a	n/a

 **Listening Lab: Example #3**

6

[e]

mid forward vowel

American English speakers are most familiar with this vowel sound as the beginning of a diphthong; however, the isolated sound can be approximated by very slowly saying the word "chaotic." The first vowel sound—before the tongue moves—is [e].

English	Italian
n/a	m<u>e</u>no

French	Latin
vr<u>ai</u>	n/a

German	Spanish
d<u>e</u>r	qu<u>e</u>

🔊 **Listening Lab: Example #4**

[ɛ]

forward vowel

Keep the lips open and the jaw relaxed.

English	Italian
b<u>e</u>d	nov<u>e</u>llo
French	**Latin**
b<u>ê</u>te	b<u>e</u>n<u>e</u>dictus
German	**Spanish**
d<u>e</u>nn	n/a

 Listening Lab: Example #5

[ə]

central vowel

Referred to as a "schwa," this symbol represents the unstressed neutral vowel sound "uh."

English	Italian
<u>a</u>bove	n/a
French	**Latin**
fill<u>e</u>	n/a
German	**Spanish**
G<u>e</u>dank<u>e</u>	n/a

🔊 Listening Lab: Example #6

forward vowel

Keep the lips parted and the jaw relaxed. English speakers often spread the lips horizontally; however, that is not necessary to produce the correct vowel sound.

English	Italian
p<u>ea</u>ce	m<u>i</u>o

French	Latin
qu<u>i</u>	k<u>y</u>r<u>i</u>e

German	Spanish
L<u>ie</u>d	ch<u>i</u>ca

 Listening Lab: Example #7

[I]

forward vowel

Keep the lips relaxed and open. Avoid nasalizing the sound when it is combined with "ng"—a common issue of English speakers.

English	Italian
p<u>i</u>t	n/a
French	**Latin**
n/a	n/a
German	**Spanish**
<u>i</u>st	n/a

Listening Lab: Example #8

[o]

back vowel

The pure vowel sound "oh" is rarely used in American English, apart from specific regions and states, such as Minnesota. It can be approximated by very slowly saying the word "dough." The first vowel sound—before the tongue moves—is [o].

English	Italian
n/a	c<u>o</u>l<u>o</u>re

French	Latin
f<u>au</u>x	n/a

German	Spanish
M<u>o</u>zart	<u>o</u>j<u>o</u>

 Listening Lab: Example #9

back vowel

Keep the lips fairly round.

English	Italian
b**ou**ght	v**o**lta
French	**Latin**
l**au**rier	gl**o**ria
German	**Spanish**
v**o**n	n/a

🔊 **Listening Lab: Example #10**

13

back vowel

Keep the lips very forward and round—more so than in regular spoken English—to pronounce this dark vowel sound.

English	Italian
f<u>oo</u>d	s<u>u</u>bito
French	**Latin**
ret<u>ou</u>r	spirit<u>u</u>m
German	**Spanish**
d<u>u</u>	az<u>u</u>l

 Listening Lab: Example #11

[ʊ]

back vowel

Allow the lips to be slightly more relaxed than [u].

English	Italian
b<u>oo</u>k	n/a
French	**Latin**
n/a	n/a
German	**Spanish**
D<u>u</u>ft	n/a

 Listening Lab: Example #12

[ʌ]

central vowel

Referred to as a "wedge," this symbol represents the stressed neutral vowel sound "uh." It is the opposite of the schwa.

English	Italian
m<u>u</u>d	n/a
French	**Latin**
n/a	n/a
German	**Spanish**
n/a	n/a

Listening Lab: Example #13

mixed vowel

This mixed vowel is produced by combining the tongue position for [i] with the lip position for [u]. To practice, say "ee" and leave the tongue in that position while rounding the lips to say "oo."

English	Italian
n/a	n/a
French	**Latin**
s<u>u</u>r	n/a
German	**Spanish**
<u>ü</u>ber	n/a

🔊 Listening Lab: Example #14

[Y]

mixed vowel

This mixed vowel is produced by combining the tongue position for [ɪ] with the lip position for [ʊ]. To practice, say "ih" and leave the tongue in that position while rounding the lips to say "uh."

English	Italian
n/a	n/a
French	**Latin**
n/a	n/a
German	**Spanish**
M<u>ü</u>tter	n/a

Listening Lab: Example #15

mixed vowel

This mixed vowel is produced by combining the tongue position for [e] with the lip position for [o]. To practice, say the first vowel sound of "chaotic" and leave the tongue in that position while rounding the lips to say "oh."

English	Italian
n/a	n/a
French	**Latin**
bl<u>eu</u>	n/a
German	**Spanish**
sch<u>ö</u>n	n/a

🔊 **Listening Lab: Example #16**

mixed vowel

This mixed vowel is produced by combining the tongue position for [ε] with the lip position for [ɔ]. To practice, say "eh" and leave the tongue in that position while rounding the lips to say "aw."

English	Italian
n/a	n/a
French	**Latin**
fl<u>eu</u>r	n/a
German	**Spanish**
G<u>ö</u>ttlich	n/a

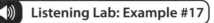

Listening Lab: Example #17

[ɛ̃]

French nasal vowel

This vowel is a nasalized version of [ɛ]. Say "eh" while allowing a small amount of air to enter the nose.

English	Italian
n/a	n/a
French	**Latin**
jard<u>in</u>	n/a
German	**Spanish**
n/a	n/a

 Listening Lab: Example #18

[ã]

French nasal vowel

This vowel is a nasalized version of [ɑ]. Say "ah" while allowing a small amount of air to enter the nose.

English	Italian
n/a	n/a
French	**Latin**
<u>en</u>f<u>an</u>t	n/a
German	**Spanish**
n/a	n/a

Listening Lab: Example #19

22

[ɔ̃]

French nasal vowel

This vowel is a nasalized version of [ɔ]. Say "aw" while allowing a small amount of air to enter the nose.

English	Italian
n/a	n/a
French	**Latin**
b<u>on</u>	n/a
German	**Spanish**
n/a	n/a

🔊 **Listening Lab: Example #20**

[õe]

French nasal vowel

This vowel is a nasalized version of [œ]. Say "eh" and leave the tongue in that position while rounding the lips to say "aw," allowing a small amount of air to enter the nose.

English	Italian
n/a	n/a
French	**Latin**
parf<u>um</u>	n/a
German	**Spanish**
n/a	n/a

Listening Lab: Example #21

diphthong

This diphthong is produced by combining [a] and [ɪ]. Quickly glide from "ah" to "ih," keeping the tip of the tongue behind the bottom front teeth.

English	Italian
h<u>igh</u>	n/a
French	**Latin**
n/a	n/a
German	**Spanish**
M<u>ai</u>	n/a

Listening Lab: Example #22

[aʊ]

diphthong

This diphthong is produced by combining [a] and [ʊ]. Quickly glide from "ah" to "uh," keeping the tip of the tongue behind the bottom front teeth.

English	Italian
c<u>ow</u>	n/a
French	**Latin**
n/a	l<u>au</u>date
German	**Spanish**
Fr<u>au</u>	fl<u>au</u>ta

 **Listening Lab: Example #23**

[oʊ]

diphthong

This diphthong is produced by combining [o] and [ʊ]. Quickly glide from "oh" to "uh," keeping the tip of the tongue behind the bottom front teeth.

English	Italian
b<u>oa</u>t	n/a
French	**Latin**
n/a	n/a
German	**Spanish**
n/a	n/a

🔊 **Listening Lab: Example #24**

[ɔɪ]

diphthong

This diphthong is produced by combining [ɔ] and [ɪ]. Quickly glide from "aw" to "ih," keeping the tip of the tongue behind the bottom front teeth.

English	Italian
b<u>oy</u>	n/a
French	**Latin**
n/a	n/a
German	**Spanish**
Fr<u>eu</u>de	v<u>oy</u>

🔊 Listening Lab: Example #25

CONSONANTS

[b]

voiced plosive consonant

Keep the lips and jaw relaxed to avoid tension.

English	Italian
<u>b</u>orn	<u>b</u>asso
French	**Latin**
<u>b</u>eau	<u>b</u>onae
German	**Spanish**
<u>B</u>itte	<u>b</u>ueno

 Listening Lab: Example #26

[ç]

voiceless fricative consonant

This is a German achlaut, although it is usually referred to as a back "ch." With the tongue in the position for the vowel sound [ɪ], emit air as if making an "h" sound.

English	Italian
n/a	n/a

French	Latin
n/a	n/a

German	Spanish
mi<u>ch</u>	n/a

Listening Lab: Example #27

[d]

voiced plosive consonant

Keep the lips and jaw relaxed to avoid tension.

English	Italian
<u>d</u>inner	<u>d</u>olce
French	**Latin**
fi<u>d</u>èle	<u>D</u>eo
German	**Spanish**
<u>d</u>as	<u>d</u>ón<u>d</u>e

 Listening Lab: Example #28

unvoiced fricative consonant

Avoid pressing. This fricative consonant should be a smooth, sustained sound.

English	Italian
<u>f</u>an	<u>f</u>orte
French	**Latin**
a<u>ff</u>aire	<u>f</u>ili
German	**Spanish**
<u>f</u>ein	<u>f</u>ino

🔊 **Listening Lab: Example #29**

[g]

voiced plosive consonant

Avoid tension by keeping the tip of the tongue behind the bottom front teeth.

English	Italian
game	spaghetti
French	**Latin**
baguette	ego
German	**Spanish**
Glas	gato

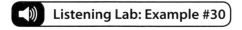 **Listening Lab: Example #30**

unvoiced fricative consonant

This unique consonant is produced by allowing air to escape through the vocal cords with the articulators already placed for the following vowel.

English	Italian
<u>h</u>at	n/a

French	Latin
n/a	n/a

German	Spanish
<u>H</u>aus	n/a

🔊 **Listening Lab: Example #31**

[ɥ]

French glide

This glide is a shortened form of [y]. Move quickly from the preceding consonant to the following vowel.

English	Italian
n/a	n/a
French	**Latin**
h<u>u</u>it	n/a
German	**Spanish**
n/a	n/a

 Listening Lab: Example #32

[j]

voiced "y" glide

Take care to avoid replacing this
sound with [dʒ] ("Could you?")
or [tʃ] ("Don't you?").

English	Italian
<u>y</u>ou	p<u>i</u>età
French	**Latin**
fi<u>ll</u>e	<u>J</u>esu
German	**Spanish**
<u>j</u>a	<u>ll</u>amar

🔊 **Listening Lab: Example #33**

37

[k]

unvoiced plosive consonant

Avoid tension by keeping the tip of the tongue behind the bottom front teeth.

English	Italian
c̲ap	c̲anto
French	**Latin**
parc̲	c̲um
German	**Spanish**
Tag̲	c̲antar

 Listening Lab: Example #34

voiced lateral consonant

Touch the tip of the tongue to the
teeth ridge.

English	Italian
love	libertà
French	**Latin**
livre	laudate
German	**Spanish**
lieben	los

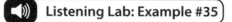

Listening Lab: Example #35

[m]

voiced nasal consonant

For full resonance, keep the jaw relaxed and the tongue forward.

English	Italian
<u>m</u>ouse	<u>m</u>io
French	**Latin**
<u>m</u>ada<u>m</u>e	do<u>m</u>inu<u>m</u>
German	**Spanish**
<u>m</u>ir	<u>m</u>adre

 **Listening Lab: Example #36**

40

voiced nasal consonant

For full resonance, keep the jaw relaxed and the tongue touching the teeth ridge.

English	Italian
<u>n</u>eat	ve<u>n</u>to
French	**Latin**
<u>n</u>eige	<u>n</u>o<u>n</u>
German	**Spanish**
<u>n</u>ei<u>n</u>	<u>n</u>úmero

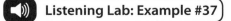

🔊 **Listening Lab: Example #37**

[ɲ]

voiced nasal consonant

Referred to as an "enya," this consonant sound is similar to [n], but is produced with the blade of the tongue instead of the tip.

English	Italian
onion	segno
French	**Latin**
baigner	agnus
German	**Spanish**
n/a	niño

🔊 **Listening Lab: Example #38**

voiced nasal consonant

For full resonance, keep the jaw dropped and the back of the tongue touching the soft palate.

English	Italian
sing	fianco
French	**Latin**
n/a	n/a
German	**Spanish**
singen	tenga

🔊 Listening Lab: Example #39

[p]

unvoiced plosive consonant

Keep the lips and jaw relaxed to avoid tension.

English	Italian
pipe	sposa
French	**Latin**
papier	pater
German	**Spanish**
ab	padre

[r]

voiced trill "r" consonant

This "r" sound is pronounced with two or more rolls of the tongue. It is not normally used in spoken English.

English	Italian
n/a	amo<u>r</u>

French	Latin
me<u>r</u>	te<u>rr</u>a

German	Spanish
He<u>rr</u>	<u>r</u>ojo

🔊 **Listening Lab: Example #41**

[ɾ]

voiced tap "r" consonant

This "r" sound is pronounced with a single tap of the tongue, similar to a light "d." American English speakers can approximate the sound by saying the word "merry" in a formal British accent.

English	Italian
n/a	ca<u>r</u>o
French	**Latin**
n/a	mise<u>r</u>ere
German	**Spanish**
Flu<u>r</u>en	pe<u>r</u>o

 Listening Lab: Example #42

[ɹ]

voiced "r" glide

This "r" sound is pronounced by moving the tongue, making it a glide. It is unique to English.

English	Italian
dairy	n/a
French	**Latin**
n/a	n/a
German	**Spanish**
n/a	n/a

[S]

unvoiced fricative consonant

Articulate this sound clearly by consciously allowing air to exit the front of the mouth between the teeth and tongue.

English	Italian
ra<u>c</u>e	<u>s</u>ei
French	**Latin**
cla<u>ss</u>e	<u>s</u>piritu
German	**Spanish**
da<u>s</u>	ro<u>s</u>a

Listening Lab: Example #44

unvoiced fricative consonant

Articulate this sound clearly by consciously allowing air to exit the front of the mouth between the teeth and tongue.

English	Italian
<u>sh</u>e	la<u>sci</u>a
French	**Latin**
<u>ch</u>at	ex<u>c</u>elsis
German	**Spanish**
<u>sch</u>ein	e<u>ch</u>ador

Listening Lab: Example #45

unvoiced plosive consonant

Keep the lips and jaw relaxed to avoid tension.

English	Italian
talk	fatale
French	**Latin**
tante	sabaoth
German	**Spanish**
Tod	tener

 Listening Lab: Example #46

unvoiced fricative consonant

This "th" consonant is called "theta."

English	Italian
ear<u>th</u>	n/a
French	**Latin**
n/a	n/a
German	**Spanish**
n/a	<u>c</u>ena

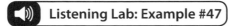

Listening Lab: Example #47

51

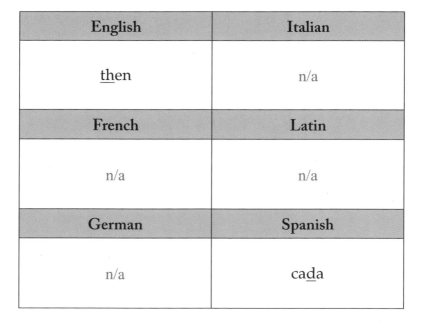

[ð]

voiced fricative consonant

This "th" consonant is called "ethe."

English	Italian
<u>th</u>en	n/a
French	**Latin**
n/a	n/a
German	**Spanish**
n/a	ca<u>d</u>a

🔊 **Listening Lab: Example #48**

voiced fricative consonant

Avoid pressing. This fricative consonant should be a smooth, sustained sound.

English	Italian
<u>v</u>oice	<u>v</u>i<u>v</u>a

French	Latin
<u>v</u>i<u>v</u>re	a<u>v</u>e

German	Spanish
<u>w</u>enn	<u>v</u>amos

🔊 **Listening Lab: Example #49**

[W]

voiced "w" glide

Keep the lips rounded.

English	Italian
<u>w</u>ent	q<u>u</u>esta

French	Latin
<u>ou</u>i	n/a

German	Spanish
n/a	g<u>u</u>erra

 Listening Lab: Example #50

voiceless fricative consonant

This is a German ichlaut, although it is usually referred to as a forward "ch." With the tongue in the position for the vowel sound [a], emit air as if making an "h" sound.

English	Italian
n/a	n/a
French	**Latin**
n/a	n/a
German	**Spanish**
Ba<u>ch</u>	n/a

🔊 **Listening Lab: Example #51**

[ʎ]

voiced approximant consonant

Referred to as an "elya," this consonant sound is similar to [l], but is produced with the blade of the tongue instead of the tip.

English	Italian
n/a	Pagliacci
French	**Latin**
n/a	n/a
German	**Spanish**
n/a	n/a

Listening Lab: Example #52

[Z]

voiced fricative consonant

Articulate this sound clearly by consciously allowing air to exit the front of the mouth between the teeth and tongue.

English	Italian
zinc	così

French	Latin
rose	Jesu

German	Spanish
singen	mismo

 Listening Lab: Example #53

[ʒ]

voiced fricative consonant

Articulate this sound clearly by consciously allowing air to exit the front of the mouth between the teeth and tongue.

English	Italian
fu<u>s</u>ion	n/a
French	**Latin**
<u>g</u>ens	n/a
German	**Spanish**
n/a	n/a

Listening Lab: Example #54

[dʒ]

voiced consonant combination

Say [d] and [ʒ] as one sound.

English	Italian
just	giovane
French	**Latin**
n/a	Regina
German	**Spanish**
n/a	inyectar

🔊 **Listening Lab: Example #55**

[gz]

voiced consonant combination

Say [g] and [z] as one sound.

English	Italian
e<u>x</u>it	n/a
French	**Latin**
e<u>x</u>hiber	e<u>x</u>alto
German	**Spanish**
n/a	n/a

Listening Lab: Example #56

[ks]

Say [k] and [s] as one sound.

English	Italian
la<u>cks</u>	n/a
French	**Latin**
a<u>cc</u>epter	n/a
German	**Spanish**
fu<u>chs</u>	e<u>x</u>haler

🔊 **Listening Lab: Example #57**

61

[kw]

voiced consonant combination

Say [k] and [w] as one sound.

English	Italian
quick	quando

French	Latin
n/a	qui

German	Spanish
n/a	cuanto

 Listening Lab: Example #58

[ts]

unvoiced consonant combination

Say [t] and [s] as one sound.

English	Italian
ca<u>ts</u>	pi<u>zz</u>a
French	**Latin**
n/a	gra<u>ti</u>a
German	**Spanish**
aben<u>ds</u>	n/a

 Listening Lab: Example #59

[t ʃ]

unvoiced consonant combination

Say [t] and [ʃ] as one sound.

English	Italian
<u>ch</u>eese	ba<u>ci</u>o
French	**Latin**
n/a	pa<u>c</u>em
German	**Spanish**
kla<u>tsch</u>	le<u>ch</u>e

 Listening Lab: Example #60